Trog and th

by Ben Butterworth
pictures by Lorraine Calaora

Nelson

'My feet are cold,' Mother said.

'My hands are cold,' Father said.

'My nose is cold,' Trog said.

'My feet **and** my hands **and** my nose are cold,' said Grandpa Gripe.

3

Father, Mother, Trog and Grandpa
were sitting in the hut.
They had no fire
and it was very cold.

'The Quickerwits
are never cold,' Mother said.
'They have fires.
Go and see how they make them.'

'I will,' Trog said.

Trog went over the hills
to the land of the Quickerwits.

They were sitting by a big fire.

'How do you make fire?' Trog asked.
'We are very cold in our huts.'

6

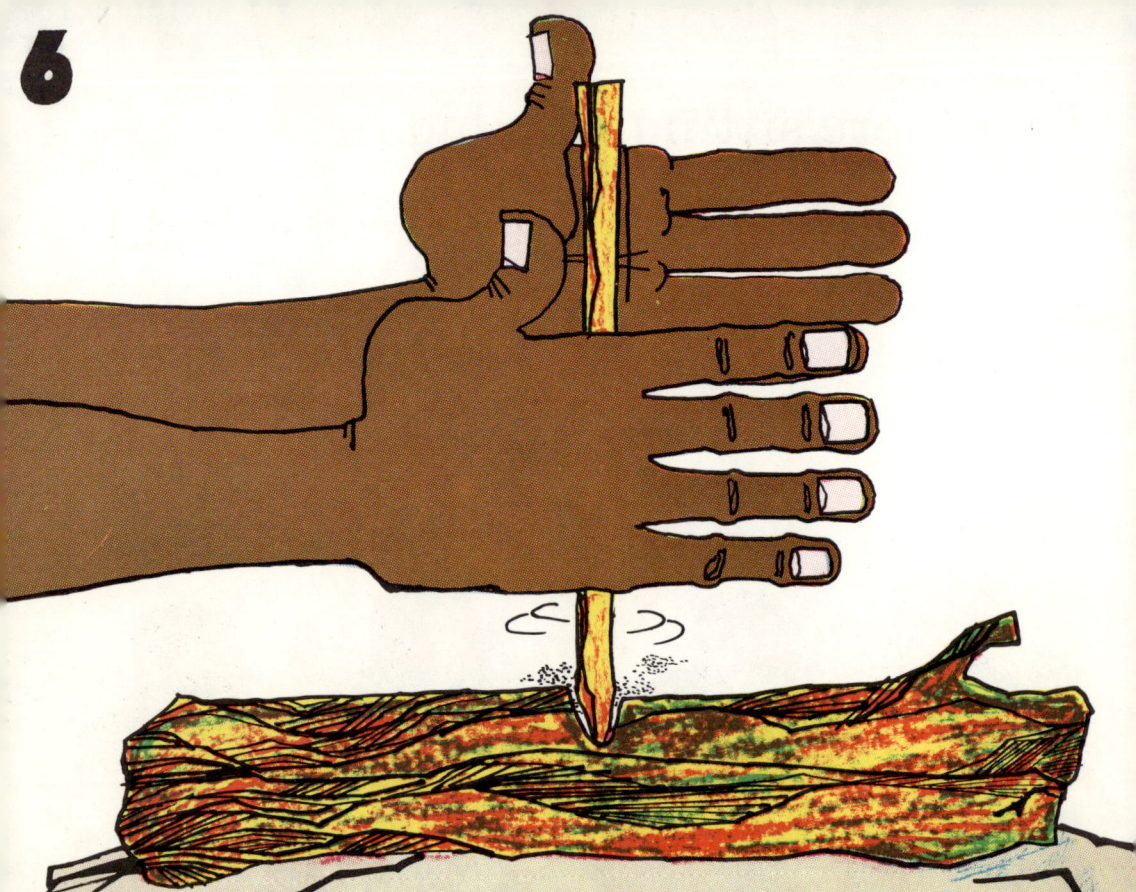

'It's easy,' the Quickerwits said.
'It's very easy!
We make a hole in a block of wood.
Then we put the sharp end of a stick
in the hole.
We roll the stick between our hands,
round and round in the hole.

Round the stick
we put dry grass and dry moss.
The rolling makes the stick hot.
The stick sets fire to the grass.
The grass sets fire to the moss.
The moss sets fire to big twigs
– and we have a fire.'

Trog went back to Father,
Mother and Grandpa Gripe.
'It's easy to make fire,' he said.
'Watch me.'

And Trog made a fire.

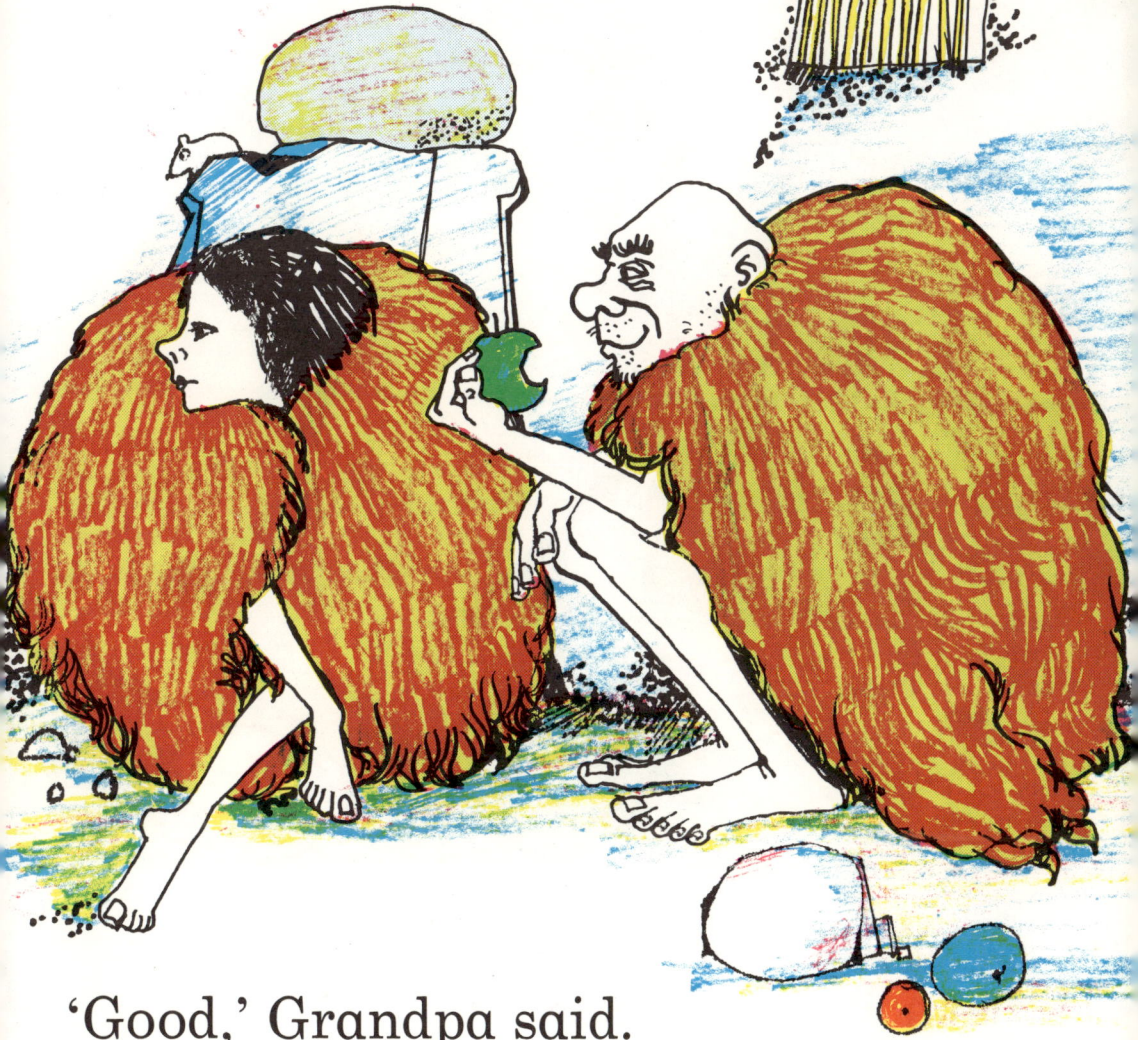

'Good,' Grandpa said.
'That's very good.
I get very cold at night.
I will have a fire in my hut.'

Grandpa took a burning branch
from Trog's fire
and made a fire in his hut.
He made the fire very big.
Then he went to sleep.

His fire burned hotter and hotter.
The smoke was blacker and blacker.
It filled the hut.
Grandpa still slept.

In the morning
Grandpa woke up
and went to
Father's hut.

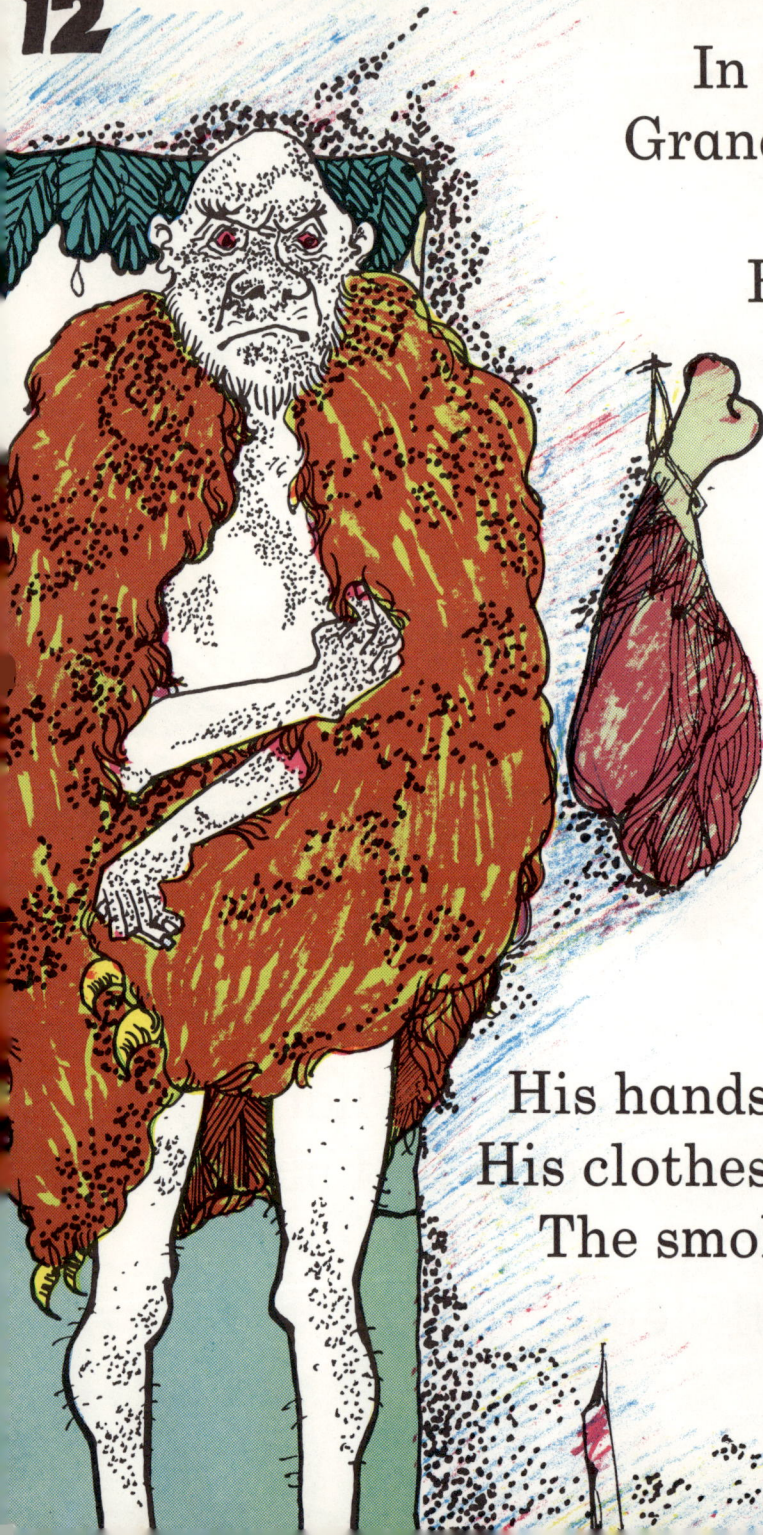

His face
was black
with smoke.
His hands were black.
His clothes were black.
The smoke had made
his eyes red.

Trog could tell it was Grandpa
but he cried,
      'Look out!
      Look out!
A black monster with red eyes
is in the hut!'

14

'Wait till the monster catches you,'
Grandpa cried,
'you and your fire and your smoke.
Wait till this monster gets you!'

'You will have to catch me,'
Trog said, and he ran off
to the land of the Quickerwits.

'Did you make a fire?'
the Quickerwits asked him.

'Yes,' Trog said, 'a good fire.'

'Did it make much smoke?'
they asked.

'Lots and **lots**,' Trog said.

'If you see
a black monster with red eyes
it will be Grandpa.'

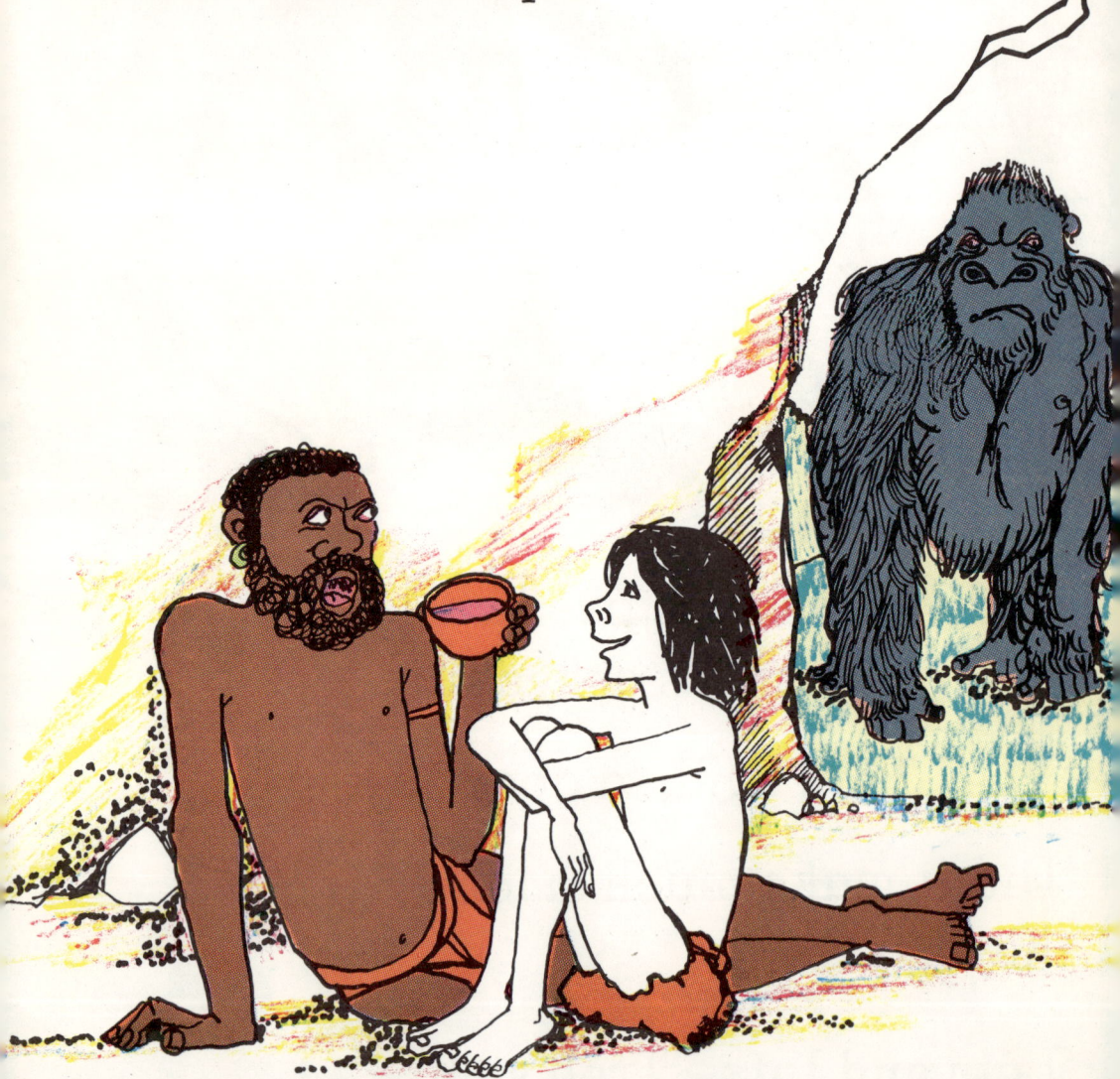